# Nature All Around
# PLANTS

Written by
## PAMELA HICKMAN

Illustrated by
## CAROLYN GAVIN

Kids Can Press

*For Riley and Isabelle Forbes from Aunt Pam — P.H.*

**Acknowledgments**

I feel so lucky to be working with Carolyn, whose beautiful illustrations brighten every page. Thank you also to my editor, Kathleen Keenan, who makes everything come together so smoothly. — *P.H.*

Big thanks to Karen Powers, the designer, who was full of direction and guidance throughout the project. Also, working with Kathleen Keenan, my editor, was seamless and a happy experience. Thanks also to my husband, Derek, for creating a beautiful studio in Belize for me to paint and a tropical garden oasis full of inspiration. — *C.G.*

Text © 2020 Pamela Hickman
Illustrations © 2020 Carolyn Gavin

Kids Can Press gratefully acknowledges the financial support of the Government of Ontario, through Ontario Creates; the Ontario Arts Council; the Canada Council for the Arts; and the Government of Canada for our publishing activity.

Published in Canada and the U.S. by Kids Can Press Ltd.
25 Dockside Drive, Toronto, ON  M5A 0B5

Kids Can Press is a Corus Entertainment Inc. company

www.kidscanpress.com

The artwork in this book was rendered in watercolor and gouache. The text is set in Kepler.

Edited by Katie Scott and Kathleen Keenan
Designed by Karen Powers

Printed and bound in Shenzhen, China, in 10/2019 by C & C Offset

FSC MIX Paper from responsible sources FSC® C008047

CM 20 0 9 8 7 6 5 4 3 2 1

**Library and Archives Canada Cataloguing in Publication**

Title: Plants / written by Pamela Hickman ; illustrated by Carolyn Gavin.

Names: Hickman, Pamela, author. | Gavin, Carolyn, illustrator.

Description: Series statement: Nature all around ; 3 | Includes index. | Based on content previously published in The kids Canadian plant book (Toronto: Kids Can Press, 1996) and Starting with nature plant book (Toronto: Kids Can Press, 1996).

Identifiers: Canadiana 2019008510X | ISBN 9781771388191 (hardcover)

Subjects: LCSH: Plants — Juvenile literature.

Classification: LCC QK49 .H53 2020 | DDC j580 — dc23

# Contents

# Plants Are All Around

Do you have plants in a garden or on your balcony? What about flowers growing in pots on your windowsill or arranged in a vase of water? When you go for a walk, do you see all kinds of plants? If you said yes to any of these questions, then plants are already part of your life.

No matter where you live, you'll find many different plants. Woodlands, fields, prairies, mountains, wetlands and shorelines are all homes to a variety of wildflowers and grasses. You'll find plants growing in crowded cities, along fences and even through sidewalk cracks. Wherever they grow, plants provide food for people and animals, offer shelter to wildlife, help keep soil from being washed away and release oxygen that people and animals need to breathe. Take a look at the different plants throughout these pages and discover more about the plants you see and depend on every day.

✳ *There are about 3800 native flowering plant species in Canada, and almost 17 000 in the United States! Learn how to identify different plants on pages 24–25.*

4

*✳ Plants use sunlight to make food in a process called photosynthesis. Find out how this works on page 9.*

*✳ Did you know that some plants eat insects? Turn to page 15 to learn more.*

*✳ Check out pages 12–13 to see how plants use their flowers to make seeds.*

*✳ Plant species that are in danger of dying out are called endangered species. Go to page 28 to find out what you can do to protect plants in your community.*

# Plants Up Close

Have you ever noticed that some plants have flowers and others don't? Those without flowers, such as ferns and mosses, are nonflowering plants. They reproduce using spores, single cells that subdivide, instead of seeds. This book looks at plants with flowers, or flowering plants, which include most of the plants you see around you. All flowering plants have four basic parts.

*LEAVES use water, sunlight and carbon dioxide from the air to make food for the plant.*

*FLOWERS produce seeds that will grow into new plants.*

*The STEM supports the plant and contains tiny tubes that carry water and food to all parts of the plant.*

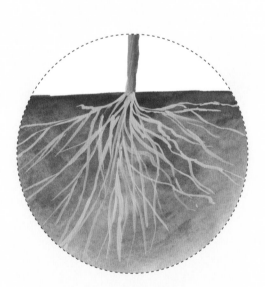

*ROOTS suck up water and minerals from the soil.*

# PLANT PROTECTION

Plants have natural defenses to discourage plant eaters. These defenses may keep people away, too.

You can see some plant defenses, such as the prickles on thistles and the thorns on wild roses, but other defenses are harder to spot. Stinging nettles have tiny, needlelike hairs on their leaves. The hairs are filled with a liquid that stings when it gets on your skin. If you've been stung, you quickly learn to recognize nettles and stay away.

Poison ivy is another plant to avoid. This woody vine or shrub grows in woodlands and along fences in the country. Look for its three leaflets and, in the fall, its white berries. The plant sap causes a very itchy rash on your skin, so don't touch! Remember the rhyme: "Leaves three, let it be. Berries white, take flight."

**FIELD THISTLE**

**PRICKLY WILD ROSE**

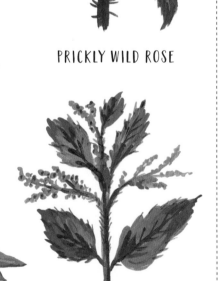

**POISON IVY**

**STINGING NETTLE**

## TWO KINDS OF PLANTS

*Plants can be divided into two groups: vascular and nonvascular. All flowering plants are vascular. They have tubelike structures, called xylem (ZIE-lem) and phloem (FLO-em), that carry food, minerals and water throughout the plant. Nonvascular plants do not have tubes and cannot transport or store water. Mosses, liverworts and hornworts are nonvascular plants.*

**CARDINAL FLOWER
(VASCULAR PLANT)**

**PRAIRIE SPHAGNUM
(NONVASCULAR PLANT)**

# A Plant's Life

Flowering plants start as seeds. A seed is like a tiny picnic basket full of food that the plant uses when it starts to grow — all that's missing is water. In spring, frozen water in the ground thaws and seeds begin to sprout, or germinate.

There are two kinds of flowering plants: monocots, such as grass, and dicots. Most garden flowers, fruits and vegetables are dicots. Watch the wheat seed and bean seed as they grow in different ways.

## WHEAT SEED (MONOCOT)

**1** *A monocot seed contains a store of food, called an endosperm, and one seed leaf, or cotyledon.*

**2** *When the seed soaks up water, it bursts. A tiny root and one leaf grow out.*

**3** *The endosperm provides food for the plant until it is big enough to make its own.*

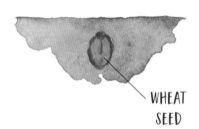

WHEAT SEED

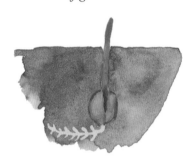

## BEAN SEED (DICOT)

**1** *A dicot seed contains two seed leaves, or cotyledons.*

**2** *When the seed germinates, the seed leaves and a tiny root burst out.*

**3** *As the plant grows, it uses up the food stored in the cotyledons. They shrivel up.*

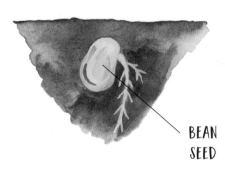

BEAN SEED

# WHY ARE LEAVES GREEN?

A plant's green leaves are filled with a chemical called chlorophyll (CLOR-o-fil). When sunlight hits a leaf, the chlorophyll absorbs the red and blue light and reflects the green part of the spectrum. You see the reflected light, making the leaf appear green. Chlorophyll plays an important part in making food for the plant in a process called photosynthesis.

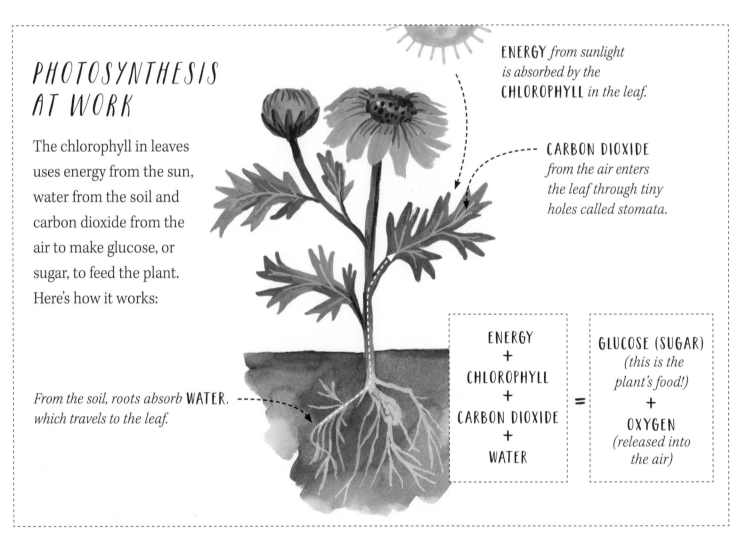

## PHOTOSYNTHESIS AT WORK

The chlorophyll in leaves uses energy from the sun, water from the soil and carbon dioxide from the air to make glucose, or sugar, to feed the plant. Here's how it works:

*From the soil, roots absorb WATER, which travels to the leaf.*

ENERGY *from sunlight is absorbed by the* CHLOROPHYLL *in the leaf.*

CARBON DIOXIDE *from the air enters the leaf through tiny holes called stomata.*

ENERGY
+
CHLOROPHYLL
+
CARBON DIOXIDE
+
WATER

=

GLUCOSE (SUGAR)
*(this is the plant's food!)*
+
OXYGEN
*(released into the air)*

# RESPIRATION

A plant's energy comes from a process called respiration. Glucose from photosynthesis is combined with oxygen, and carbon dioxide is released. This is the opposite of what happens in photosynthesis. Plants respire all the time, even at night.

# Looking at Flowers

Take a look at the flowers in your neighborhood. You'll see a rainbow of colors and lots of different shapes and sizes. If you get nose-to-nose with some flowers, you can smell their sweet scents. People have enjoyed flowers for thousands of years, but the colors, shapes and fragrances of flowers are really designed to attract pollinators, including birds, bats and insects such as honeybees.

*Some flowers have hidden colors or patterns that we can't see. These flowers absorb ultraviolet light from the sun, which creates color patterns only bees can see. These patterns show bees where the flower's nectar is stored. Compare how you and a bee see this common evening primrose.*

WHAT HUMANS SEE          WHAT BEES SEE

*Tubelike flowers, especially red ones, often have lots of nectar, a favorite food of hummingbirds. The long-tubed flowers of a scarlet bee balm are the perfect shape for ruby-throated hummingbirds. They use their long beaks and tongues to pump nectar out of the flowers.*

RUBY-THROATED
HUMMINGBIRD

SCARLET
BEE BALM

Some flowers, such as honeysuckle, jasmine and sweet rocket, release their scents late in the evening to attract animals that are active at night. Moths and bats are attracted to the scents of these flowers.

SWEET ROCKET

WHITE-LINED SPHINX MOTH

Flat flowers, such as yarrow, asters and daisies, are easiest for butterflies to land on. Butterflies taste with their feet and use their long tongues to suck up nectar from the flowers.

Did you know that trees are a kind of plant? Most trees have flowers. They also have thick, woody stems and grow much bigger than the soft-stemmed plants in this book. Like most plants, trees have roots, stems and leaves (or needles).

VARIABLE CHECKERSPOT BUTTERFLY

SEASIDE DAISY

BLACK COTTONWOOD

11

# Plants in Spring

One of the most exciting things about spring is discovering tiny green shoots poking through the soil where the snow has just melted. Flowers that bloom in spring can tolerate cold nights and a few late snowfalls. Their blooming period happens just as insect pollinators become active again. Early flowers receive many visits from pollinators because there is little competition from other plants. They are able to flower and produce seeds quickly.

# POLLINATION

A plant's flowers make seeds, which will grow into new plants. If you look closely, you'll see the male and female parts flowers need to produce seeds in a process called pollination. Pollination means that a flower's pollen is transferred from the stamen (the male part of a plant) to the pistil (the female part of a plant). Flowers are pollinated by wind and animals.

**1** *A bee visits the swamp rose mallow. As it feeds, tiny grains of pollen from the flower's stamen get stuck to the bee's feet and body.*

STAMEN

PISTIL

**2** *The bee visits another swamp rose mallow. Some of the pollen drops onto the second flower's sticky pistil.*

**3** *The pollen grains germinate and release the male reproductive cells. These travel down the pistil to unite with the egg cells inside the flower's ovary. This is called fertilization.*

OVARY

SEED HEAD

**4** *Once the flower is fertilized, seeds develop inside the ovary. The petals dry up and fall off, and the ovary turns into the seed head.*

SEEDS

**5** *Eventually, the seeds will fall to the ground, where they may grow into new swamp rose mallow plants in the spring.*

## STRANGE PLANTS

*Wild rice is a wind-pollinated grass that grows in North America. Flowers that are pollinated by wind don't need to attract animals. Like the flowers of most grasses, wild rice flowers are colorless, odorless and nectarless. They grow on spikes to make it easier to release their pollen to the breeze.*

WILD RICE

# Plants in Summer

Wildflowers bloom at different times throughout the summer. You can find them in fields and hedgerows and along roadsides. Some flowers even grow in water. Each kind of flower is adapted to bloom according to the temperature and amount of daylight in its environment. As long as there is enough rain, the plants will grow, flower and produce seeds.

As summer progresses, you can find the seed heads of some early bloomers, such as wild lupines and dandelions, alongside the flowers of later plants, such as wild carrot and goldenrod.

# INSECT-EATING PLANTS

If you don't like swatting away bugs in summer, you'll be happy to discover that some plants trap and digest them. Insect-eating plants usually grow in soils without a lot of nutrients. These plants get extra nutrition, especially nitrogen, from eating bugs.

**BUTTERWORT**

*The butterwort has flat, sticky leaves that attract insects. Once an insect is stuck to it, the leaf's edges roll inward to cover the insect. Inside the trap, the insect is digested.*

*The pitcher plant has jug-shaped leaves with edges coated in a slippery, waxlike substance. When an insect lands on a leaf, it slides right into the liquid-filled pitcher below. Long, downward-pointing hairs stop the insect from crawling out. The insect drowns and is soon digested by the plant.*

**PITCHER PLANT**

**SUNDEW**

*The Venus flytrap doesn't really come from the planet Venus — it grows in North and South Carolina in the United States. It has hinged leaves with long, sensitive bristles. When an insect brushes against a leaf, the leaf snaps shut like a clam, trapping its dinner inside.*

**VENUS FLYTRAP**

*The sundew has long rays of hairs tipped with a glue-like substance, resembling dewdrops. Insects that land on the sundew get stuck on the hairs and can't get free. The hairy leaves close over them like a temporary stomach, and then they are absorbed.*

15

# Plants in Fall

By fall, many flowers have been replaced by seeds. Seeds have hard shells, called seed coats, that protect them from extreme weather during cold or dry seasons.

When the weather gets warm again in spring, the seeds will sprout and grow into new plants. Some flowers produce thousands of seeds, so there is a better chance they will survive.

✳ *In fall, farmers harvest the seeds of many plants for food. Grains such as wheat, barley, rye and oats, as well as corn, are all important parts of our diet.*

# SPREADING SEEDS

The seeds of wild plants can spread in many amazing ways. Seeds sail on the wind, float in the water or hitch a ride on an animal. Seeds have to spread out so that they are not competing with each other for the soil, water and sunshine they need to grow. Many seeds don't land in the right spot, and so they never grow.

**JEWELWEED**

*Jewelweeds, or touch-me-nots, grow in damp woodlands. In late summer, look for a long, narrow, bulging seedpod, a pouch-like structure containing the plant's seeds. Gently squeeze it between your thumb and first finger. The seedpod will immediately burst and coil up, throwing the seeds through the air.*

*The tiny seeds on sweet wild strawberries are hard to digest, so animals excrete them, often a long way from where the berries were growing. This is how strawberry seeds get "planted" in new areas.*

**WILD STRAWBERRIES**

**COMMON MILKWEED**

*The sticky seeds, stems and leaves of cleavers are covered in hooked hairs. In the summer, these parts of the cleaver catch on passing animals, and the seeds hitch a ride to a new growing place.*

*In late summer and early fall, common milkweed plants ripen and their large, fat seedpods split open. Each little brown seed is attached to a bit of fluff that carries it on the wind like a parachute.*

**CLEAVER**

# Plants in Winter

How do plants survive icy-cold winters in the north? Like many animals, plants hibernate, or rest, during winter. When the killing frosts of fall arrive, the stems and flowers of most plants die.

You can find the dried stalks of winter wildflowers in open fields or along roadsides and fences. Wildflowers produce seeds that fall to the ground and spend winter safe inside their tough seed coats. When warm weather thaws the ground, the seeds soak up water from the soil until they burst from their seed coats. Shoots and roots grow out, and soon they will grow flowers.

# ALIVE IN THE COLD

Perennials are plants that come back year after year, such as wild carrots and trilliums. These plants don't die completely in the fall. Instead, perennials have underground roots or bulbs that survive the winter and send up new shoots when the warm weather returns. Some perennials also leave a ring, or rosette, of ground-hugging leaves under the snow. New growth sprouts up through these leaves in spring.

WILD CARROT

TRILLIUM

# EARLY BLOOMERS

Plants called annuals, such as marigolds and petunias, flower early in the spring and keep blooming all summer, then produce seeds. Annuals die completely in the cold, but the seeds of some can survive cold winters in the soil and produce new plants in the spring. Most annuals have to be replanted each year.

MARIGOLD

PETUNIA

## STRANGE PLANTS

Eastern skunk cabbage can generate its own heat and melt its way through the frozen ground in early spring. It flowers while ice and snow are still around. The skunk cabbage's name comes from the odor it produces. The smell attracts insects such as scavenger flies, which feed on dead animals, and other pollinators.

EASTERN SKUNK CABBAGE

19

# Growing Zones

If you were planting a garden in southern California, you would grow different plants than someone planting a garden in northern New Brunswick. That's because different regions in Canada and the United States have different climates and growing conditions. Each plant is adapted to its growing zone, or the area where it grows best. Some plants can tolerate the cold, and some grow only in warm areas. Some can survive very dry conditions, while others need lots of rain. The map shows the different growing zones in Canada and the United States.

In tropical countries, where the climate is warm year-round with lots of rainfall, many kinds of plants grow much bigger than they do in Canada and most of the United States.

CANADA

UNITED STATES

| Growing Zones | Common Plant Species |
|---|---|
| 0 | *sedge* |
| 1 | *Arctic poppy, Arctic lupine, mountain avens, pasqueflower* |
| 2 | *Kalm's lobelia, northern bog aster, northern willowherb* |
| 3 | *Canada anemone, blue columbine, field pussytoes* |
| 4 | *Missouri goldenrod, blue giant hyssop, Macoun's buttercup* |
| 5 | *common St. Johnswort, New England aster, Michigan lily* |
| 6 | *wild bergamot, hollow Joe-Pye weed, pink lady's-slipper* |
| 7 | *butterfly weed, cardinal flower, Virginia bluebells* |
| 8 | *calendula, black-eyed Susan, coreopsis* |
| 9 | *dense blazing star, candytuft, swamp rose mallow* |
| 10 | *blue flax, penstemon, blanketflower* |
| 11 | *passionflower, calla lily, liatris* |
| 12 | *red ginger, anthurium, bamboo orchid* |

ALASKA

HAWAII

# Plant Habitats

Canada and the United States are made up of many different habitats. A habitat is a place where plants and animals live. Each habitat has a climate and soils that suit the plants that grow there.

✳ *Aquatic plants have special ways of getting air to their waterlogged roots. Most plants have their stomata on the underside of their leaves to reduce water loss. But water lilies have floating leaves with stomata on top so the plant can get more air. Water lilies also have channels in their stems that carry air to their roots.*

WATER LILY

PASQUEFLOWER

✳ *Arctic and alpine plants, such as pasqueflowers, face cold, dry and often windy climates and a short growing season. They must go through their entire life cycle before they are killed by early frosts. They grow quickly and close to the ground, often clumped together. Their hairy leaves prevent water loss and provide insulation from the cold.*

✻ Western wild bergamot is a prairie plant that has adapted to deal with low rainfall and strong winds by growing in tight clusters. Each fall, stems and leaves from dead plants form a thick layer over the ground that helps stop soil from drying out or blowing away.

WESTERN WILD BERGAMOT

✻ Heavy rainfall, warm temperatures and a long growing season help tropical and subtropical plants grow quickly. Tropical plants, such as red ginger, undergo a dry season and a wet season. During the wet season, plants grow, flower and produce seeds. In the dry season, the plants rest and their leaves may turn brown and drop off.

RED GINGER

✻ Desert plants, such as prickly pear, a type of cactus, have to find and store water to survive. A cactus's spikes are really modified leaves that lose less water than larger leaves and protect the plant from plant eaters. Many desert plants also have special seeds that can wait years for rain.

PRICKLY PEAR

✻ In spring, woodland plants on the forest floor grow quickly, before the tree leaves come out and shade the plants from sunlight. Wildflowers such as spring beauty have only a few weeks to grow, flower, make seeds and store enough food in their underground roots and bulbs for next year.

SPRING BEAUTY

# Beginner Plant-Watching

You can find plants to watch at any time of year. Remember to watch them in their natural habitats instead of picking them. Use this checklist and a field guide to help identify the plants in your neighborhood.

## FLOWERS

- Are they regular or irregular?

*regular*     *irregular*

- Do they have a stalk or no stalk?

*stalk*     *no stalk*

- Are they solitary or composite (made up of many small flowers)?

*solitary*     *composite*

- What shape are they?

*tubular*     *bell-shaped*

*cup-shaped*     *spiked*

- What color and size are they?

## LEAVES

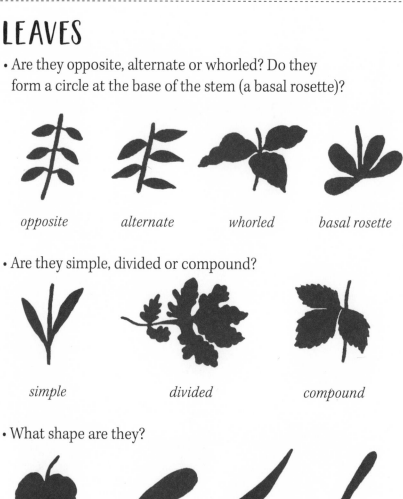

- Are they opposite, alternate or whorled? Do they form a circle at the base of the stem (a basal rosette)?

*opposite*     *alternate*     *whorled*     *basal rosette*

- Are they simple, divided or compound?

*simple*     *divided*     *compound*

- What shape are they?

*heart-shaped*     *oval*     *lance-shaped*     *linear*

## SEEDS

- What shape, size and color are the seeds and seedpods?
- Are the seeds sticky or smooth?

## STEMS

- Are they long or short?
- Are they round, square or triangular?
- Are they hairy, smooth or prickly?
- Are they simple or branching?

## HABITAT

- Are the plants growing in water, in woodlands, in a desert, on a mountain?
- Are they growing in sun or in shade?

CAMERA

MAGNIFYING GLASS

FIELD GUIDE

NOTEBOOK

PENCIL

## POISONOUS PLANTS

Always check with an adult before eating wild plants. Some plants look harmless but are very poisonous to people and animals. Other plants have poisonous seeds or leaves.

- All parts of these plants are poisonous.

*belladonna*　　　*foxglove*

- These plants have poisonous seeds.

*lupine*　　*larkspur*　　*monkshood*　　*sweet pea*

- This plant has poisonous leaves.

*rhubarb*

# More Strange Plants

## UP A TREE

*FLORIDA*

The cigar orchid is a type of epiphyte (EP-ee-fite), a plant that grows on another plant. It uses a tree for support only and takes nutrients from the rainwater that flows down the tree bark. Cigar orchids grow on swamp trees, such as cypress and buttonwood.

CIGAR ORCHID

## SPREADS LIKE WILDFIRE

*SOUTH OF THE ARCTIC CIRCLE TO GEORGIA*

The tall, pinkish-red flowers of fireweed are common in burned or cleared areas. Fireweed quickly colonizes open areas and thrives as long as there is enough light. After about five years, fireweed dies out, but its seeds remain in the soil. If another forest fire burns the area, the seeds can germinate and recolonize the habitat.

FIREWEED

## GOT MILK?

*EASTERN AND SOUTHERN U.S., CANADIAN PRAIRIES AND EASTERN CANADA*

Common milkweed gets its name from its white sap, which can be toxic to people and animals. Many insects are attracted to the nectar of the flowers. The monarch butterfly depends on the common milkweed for survival. Adults lay their eggs on the plant, and caterpillars feed exclusively on its leaves.

COMMON MILKWEED

# TOUCH ME NOT

*SOUTHERN U.S. AND HAWAII*

The sensitive plant has a unique way of defending itself from harm. Its compound leaves fold up and droop when it is touched, blown on or exposed to heat. The sensitive plant also closes at night and reopens in the morning. Botanists think that the sudden movement may scare off plant eaters, dislodge harmful insects or conserve water.

SENSITIVE PLANT

# ALL ABOUT WATER

*ARIZONA*

The saguaro is a type of cactus that has developed special features to help it survive in the desert. Its thick waterproof skin prevents water loss, and its large spines keep animals from stealing the water supply it has stored inside. The saguaro's stem is pleated so it can expand and absorb as much rain as possible. It also has a deep taproot that can reach 1.5 m (5 ft.) underground to find stored water.

SAGUARO

# TINY APPLES

*EASTERN NORTH AMERICA*

The mayapple is a woodland plant that grows in early spring. A single flower grows below a pair of large, umbrellalike leaves. It produces an edible yellow apple-like berry that can be used in jams, jellies and pies. Plants without flowers only produce one leaf.

MAYAPPLE

# Endangered Plants

When a meadow is plowed under, a forest is cut down or a marsh is filled in, the plants in these habitats are destroyed. The plants may even become endangered, which means they must be helped or they will become extinct. When plants become extinct, there are no more of them growing anywhere in the world.

Habitat loss is the main reason some plants, such as California jewelflowers, are endangered. The invasion of new plants that aren't naturally found in a habitat can also endanger plants that already live there. Purple loosestrife was introduced into North American marshes and grew quickly, crowding out native plants. Other plants are endangered due to overpicking.

Fortunately, scientists are fighting back. They're experimenting with a beetle that eats only purple loosestrife. Some endangered plants are protected by laws or kept safe in national, provincial and state parks and nature reserves. Conservation groups also work to protect native plants and their habitats.

You can help to protect the plants in your community by following a few simple steps:

✳ Tell your family and friends why plants are important in nature.

✳ Enjoy wild plants in their natural habitats instead of picking them or digging them up.

✳ Stay on paths and hiking trails in parks so you don't trample plants.

✳ Help take care of the plants in your yard or at school.

CALIFORNIA JEWELFLOWER

PURPLE LOOSESTRIFE

# GROW MICROGREENS

*Microgreens are the stems and small leaves of plants, picked before they are fully grown. You can grow microgreens to eat in salads and sandwiches any time of year. They are packed with important vitamins and nutrients.*

### YOU'LL NEED:

- spinach, radish or beet seeds
- water
- a bowl
- a shallow tray, such as a baking dish
- organic potting soil
- scissors
- spray bottle

**1** Soak seeds in a bowl of water overnight to speed up germination.

**2** Place 2.5 cm (1 in.) of soil in the bottom of the tray and smooth it out. Scatter the seeds evenly over the soil.

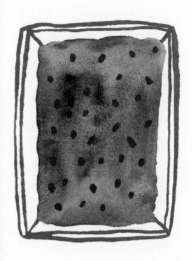

**3** Cover the seeds with a thin layer of soil and gently spray the surface with water.

**4** Place the tray near a sunny window. Mist the seeds with water a few times a day to keep the soil moist all over.

**5** When the first true leaves appear and the greens are 2.5 to 5 cm (1 to 2 in.) tall, they are ready to harvest. This takes two to four weeks, depending on the kind of seed. Use scissors to cut the stems close to the soil's surface. Eat the stems and leaves, and reuse the soil to grow more microgreens.

# Glossary

**annual:** a plant that blooms from spring until late fall but dies completely in the cold

**chlorophyll:** the green pigment found in plants

**cotyledon:** the first leaf or leaves that come out of a seed when it germinates. They are sometimes called seed leaves.

**dicot:** a plant whose seed contains two seed leaves, or cotyledons. Most garden flowers, fruits and vegetables are dicots.

**egg cell:** the female reproductive cell in a flower. When it unites with the male cell from pollen, it produces a seed.

**endangered species:** a species that could become extinct, or die out completely, if the threats to its survival are not controlled or reversed

**endosperm:** a store of food inside the seed of a monocot

**epiphyte:** a plant that grows on another plant but only for support. Examples include some ferns, bromeliads and orchids in tropical rainforests.

**fertilization:** the union of the male and female reproductive cells of flowers to form a seed

**germinate:** to begin to grow or develop

**glucose:** a type of sugar produced during photosynthesis

**habitat:** the natural home or environment where an animal, plant or other organism lives

**monocot:** a plant whose seed contains an endosperm and one seed leaf, or cotyledon. Grass is an example of a monocot.

**nectar:** a high-calorie, sugary liquid produced by flowering plants. It provides food and energy to pollinators.

**nonvascular plant:** a plant with no tubelike vessels so it cannot retain water or transport it to other parts of the plant. Mosses, liverworts and hornworts are nonvascular plants.

**ovary:** the part of the pistil where fertilization takes place and seeds form

**perennial:** a plant that comes back year after year and does not die completely in the fall

**phloem:** plant tissue that contains tubelike vessels that transport food from the leaves to the rest of the plant

**photosynthesis:** a chemical process in green plants that uses light energy to combine water and carbon dioxide to produce glucose and oxygen

**pistil:** the female part of a flower made up of the stigma, style and ovary

**pollen:** a powderlike substance from a flower that contains a plant's male reproductive cells

**pollination:** the transfer of pollen from a flower's stamen to the pistil of the same or a different flower

**respiration:** the chemical process that converts glucose and oxygen into carbon dioxide and water to produce energy for the plant

**sap:** the liquid inside a plant that contains sugars and minerals dissolved in water. It flows between the roots and the leaves.

**seed:** the result of the union of the male and female reproductive cells of plants during pollination. Under the right conditions, the cells inside a seed will produce the root and stem of a new plant.

**seed coat:** the hard outer shell that protects a seed from weather and other damage

**stalk:** a part of some plants that branches off from the main stem to support another part of the plant, such as a leaf or flower

**stamen:** the male part of a flower, made up of the anther and filament

**stomata:** tiny pores mainly on the underside of leaves. They open during photosynthesis to let air in and extra water and oxygen out.

**taproot:** a large, central carrot-shaped root, out of which smaller roots grow

**vascular plant**: a plant that contains the tubelike structures xylem and phloem to transport water and nutrients. All flowering plants are vascular.

**xylem:** plant tissue that contains tubelike vessels that transport water and nutrients from the roots to the leaves

31

# Index